Blind Tom

The Horse Who Helped
Build the Great Railroad

Blind Tom

THE HORSE WHO HELPED BUILD THE GREAT RAILROAD

Shirley Raye Redmond

ILLUSTRATED BY

Lois Bradley

 Mountain Press
PUBLISHING COMPANY
MISSOULA, MONTANA
2009

Library of Congress Cataloging-in-Publication Data

Redmond, Shirley-Raye, 1955-
  Blind Tom : the horse who helped build the great railroad / Shirley
Raye Redmond ; illustrated by Lois Bradley.
      p. cm.
  ISBN 978-0-87842-558-7 (pbk. : alk. paper)
  1. Pacific railroads—Juvenile literature. 2. Horses—Juvenile literature. 3. Working animals—Juvenile literature. I. Bradley, Lois,
1960- ill. II. Title.
  TF25.P23R43 2009
  625.1'40973--dc22
                        2009009759

                PRINTED IN HONG KONG

MP **Mountain Press**
PUBLISHING COMPANY
P.O. BOX 2399 • MISSOULA, MT 59806
406-728-1900 • www.mountain-press.com

For my loveys,
Wyatt, Cheyenne, and Dakota

—SHIRLEY RAYE REDMOND

❖ ❖ ❖ ❖ ❖ ❖ ❖

For Jeff, Kat, and Ry

—LOIS BRADLEY

This is the story

of a real horse who lived long ago, in the 1860s. The horse was called Blind Tom because he could not see. Although he was blind, he was strong and smart, and he could work. He pulled flatcars full of rails, spikes, and tools. His work helped people build the Great Railroad.

What do you suppose the Great Railroad
was used for?

Traveling!

Before the Great Railroad was built, going between the eastern states, like New York and Pennsylvania, to the western states, like California and Oregon, took a long, long time. Back then, there were no cars or airplanes. Travelers had to sail on ships all the way around South America, or they had to ride hundreds of miles across the country in wagons pulled by horses, mules, or oxen. The trip took many months.

What do you suppose would go faster than a ship or a wagon?

A train!

Trains could go much faster, but there were no railroad tracks that went all the way across the country. The tracks started on the East Coast but stopped at the Mississippi River.

So the president, Abraham Lincoln, decided to build the Great Railroad. The tracks would go from the Mississippi River to California. When it was finished, people would be able to travel from east to west, and from west to east, in just a few days.

The American people liked President Lincoln's plan. They were very excited to think that they would soon have a new railroad to take them across the country so quickly. But building a railroad was very hard work.

Who do you suppose would build the railroad?

Workers!

Thousands of workers were hired to build the Great Railroad. Some were veterans of the Civil War. Others came from China, Ireland, and other faraway countries to live in America and help lay the new tracks.

But the workers needed help. They had to move heavy iron rails and spikes, which were piled onto flatcars. The cars were very hard to pull.

What do you suppose could help pull the flatcars?

Horses!

The railroad workers brought in many, many horses. The workers put the cars on the tracks and hitched them to the horses. Then the horses pulled the cars to the place where the new tracks were being laid. The men chose the strongest and smartest horse to be the leader.

Which horse do you suppose that was?

Blind Tom!

Every morning, a man hitched Tom to the first flatcar full of iron rails and spikes. When the flatcar was ready, the man gave Tom a firm pat on his flank and said, "Giddyup!" Tom knew what to do. He galloped to the end of the track.

Workers called "iron men" waited at the end of the track for Tom and his load. When he arrived, the men cried, "Whoa!" and Tom stopped. Tom waited patiently as the men lifted the rails from his car one at a time.

What do you suppose Tom did as he waited?

He listened!

When the crew boss shouted, "Down!" Tom heard the men drop the rail into place with a loud thud:

Plonk!

Then the men with hammers pounded in the spikes. It was very noisy:

Clang, clang, clang!

The workers lifted each rail one by one.

Each time, they made the same sounds over

and over again.

"Down!"

Plonk!

Clang, clang, clang!

"Down!"

Plonk!

Clang, clang, clang!

To Blind Tom, it was like a song. The song

did not stop until the car was empty.

When Blind Tom's flatcar was empty, the workers pushed it off the track. Blind Tom returned to the end of the line, and the horse behind him moved forward with a new load.

At the end of the line, Tom waited for the workers to hitch a new, full flatcar to his harness. When they said, "Giddyup," he hurried back to the iron men again. There he listened to another clanging song.

All day long, Tom went back and forth, back and forth along the railroad tracks. As he did, something good was happening.

What do you suppose it could be?

The tracks were growing !

Each day, the tracks grew longer and longer. The men and animals worked for years. The workers knew that the railroad could not be built without Tom and the other horses.

"Tom works as hard as we do," a man said.

Everyone agreed.

Bad weather made the work even harder. In the winter, snow and ice made the ground slippery. Cold winds sometimes hurt Blind Tom's eyes and ears. He had to pull extra hard to drag his flatcar through the heavy snow. This made him tired and sore.

In the spring, rain and melting snow sometimes
made the rivers flood. Blind Tom had to pull his
car through the deep mud. Once in a while, he
even got stuck. Getting stuck is scary for a horse.
But soon the workers came to help him.

One day, a newspaper reporter was watching the workers build the railroad. He saw the flatcars full of rails and spikes. He saw the horses pulling them. The reporter wrote stories about the railroad for people to read in the newspaper. Blind Tom was in the stories, too. Soon, Blind Tom was a little bit famous!

Each day, telegraph operators sent a message to the railroad workers asking how long the track had grown. The operators had read the newspaper stories about Blind Tom. They knew that wherever Tom was, that was how far the railroad tracks stretched.

So instead of asking the workers how many miles of track they had laid, what do you suppose they asked?

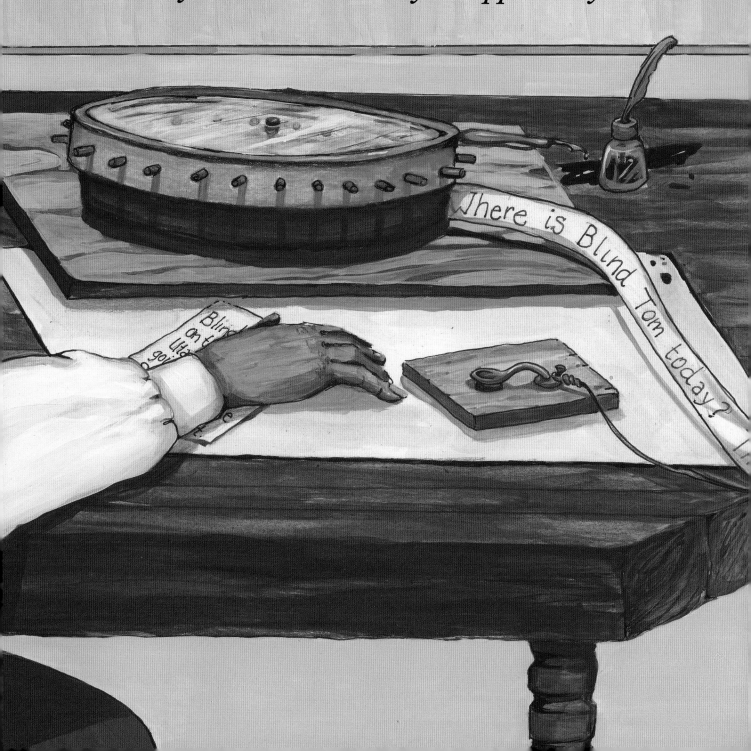

They asked,

"Where's Blind Tom today?"

At last, the railroad workers finished the tracks. The job had taken six years. In that time, the workers had built almost 2,000 miles of track.

To celebrate, the railroad companies held a special "golden spike" ceremony. On May 10, 1869, people from all over the United States met in a big field, high in the Promontory Mountains of Utah.

Everyone came to watch the railroad chiefs pound in the last spike, which was made of gold. Both of the men missed when they tried to hit the golden spike with their hammer. Everyone laughed.

One of the railroad men finally hammered in the last spike:

Clang, clang, clang!

The sound was very familiar to Blind Tom. But this time, instead of hearing, "Down! Plonk!" all he heard was the cheering of the crowd.

A telegraph operator sent the good news to the world. He wrote only one word:

Done!

A photographer took a picture of the railroad workers in front of the train tracks.

Who do you suppose was also in the picture?

Blind Tom!

He stood in the back with his friends, the iron men.

This was the end of Blind Tom's hard work, but it was a new beginning for America.

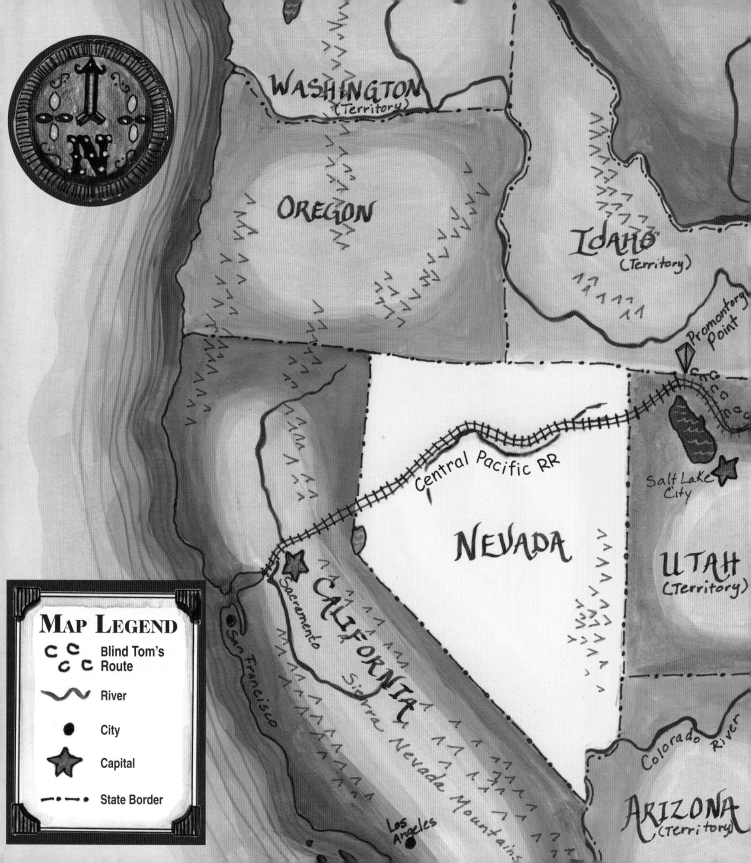

WASHINGTON
(Territory)

OREGON

IDAHO
(Territory)

Promontory
Point

Central Pacific RR

Salt Lake
City

NEVADA

UTAH
(Territory)

Sacramento

CALIFORNIA

San Francisco

Sierra Nevada Mountains

Colorado River

Los Angeles

ARIZONA
(Territory)

MAP LEGEND

C C
C C   Blind Tom's Route

〰   River

●   City

★   Capital

·—·—·   State Border

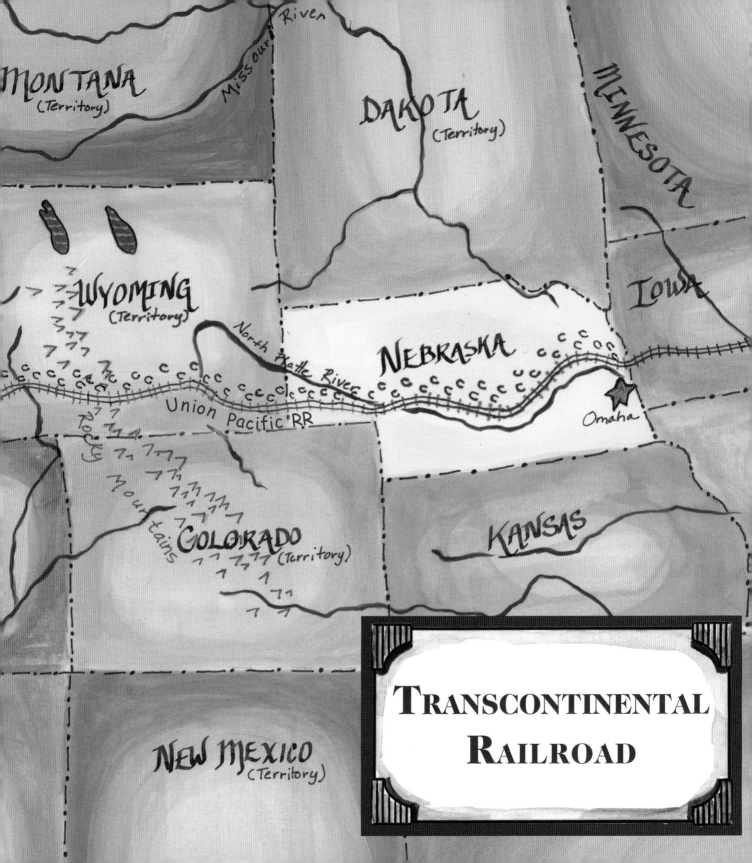

Things to Know

1869: The year the Great Railroad was finished. To see how long ago this was, subtract 1869 from the year it is now.

Abraham Lincoln: The president of the United States during the American Civil War in the 1860s. He asked for the Great Railroad to be built, but he died four years before it was finished.

ceremony: A kind of show that is put on to celebrate a big event.

flatcar: A railcar that has an open platform without sides or a roof.

harness: A set of leather straps fitted to a horse or other draft animal so that it can be attached to and pull a wagon, carriage, flatcar, or other load.

transcontinental railroad: A railway that crosses an entire continent, usually from "sea to sea," connecting the east coast with the west coast. The Great Railroad was the first transcontinental railroad in the world.

spike: A large, heavy nail used to fasten the rails to a railroad tie.

telegraph: A machine used to send messages across a great distance. People used this machine before the telephone was invented.

veteran: A person who served in the armed forces during a war.

Learn More About the Great Railroad

Explore America's railroad heritage at the National Railroad Museum, 22285 S. Broadway, Green Bay, Wisconsin, or visit the museum's Web site: www.nationalrrmuseum.org.

Find amazing photos, information, and more at the Central Pacific Railroad Photographic History Museum, a virtual museum: http://cprr.org/.

Visit the Union Pacific Railroad Museum in person at 200 Pearl Street, Council Bluffs, Iowa, or on the Web at: www.uprr.com/aboutup/history/.

To find out about the annual reenactment of the Golden Spike Ceremony, visit the Golden Spike Historic Site, north of Salt Lake City, Utah, or check out their Web site: www.nps.gov/archive/gosp/home.html.

Want to read the true story of Chief Spotted Tail and his race against the Iron Horse? Visit Shirley Raye Redmond's Web site, www.readshirleyraye.com, and click on "Blind Tom."

Bibliography

Ambrose, Stephen E. *Nothing Like It in the World: The Men Who Built the Transcontinental Railroad, 1863–1869*. New York: Simon & Schuster, 2000.

Harter, Jim. *American Railroads of the Nineteenth Century: A Pictorial History in Victorian Woodcuts*. Lubbock: Texas Tech University Press, 1998.

Howard, Robert West. *The Horse in America*. Chicago and New York: Follett Publishing Company, 1965.

Jensen, Oliver. *The American Heritage History of Railroads in America*. New York: Bonanza Books, 1975.

Stover, John F. *American Railroads*. 2nd ed. Chicago: University of Chicago Press, 1997.

Williams, John Hoyt. *The Great and Shining Road: The Epic Story of the Transcontinental Railroad*. New York: Times Books/Random House, 1988.

About the Author

Shirley Raye Redmond took her first cross-country train ride at the age of eighteen months, followed by an ocean voyage. She grew up on the island of Okinawa, Japan. After earning a master's degree in literature from the University of Illinois, Springfield, she settled in New Mexico, where she worked for many years as a teacher.

Shirley Raye is the author of several nonfiction books for children, including *Lewis & Clark: A Prairie Dog for the President* (Random House) and *Pigeon Hero!* (Simon & Schuster). She lives in Los Alamos, New Mexico, with her husband, Bill, and a rambunctious Scottie named Duncan.

Visit her Web site at www.readshirleyraye.com.

About the Illustrator

Lois Bradley lives with her family in the mountains outside of Albuquerque, New Mexico, with two dogs, two cats, many fish, and a tarantula. Lois, her husband, Jeff, and her daughter and son all spend as much time as possible outdoors. The family loves kayaking, mountain biking, hiking, camping, and roaming throughout the Southwest.

Lois grew up in Emporia, Kansas, and attended Kansas State University, Emporia State University, and Central New Mexico Community College. She is currently a full-time art student at the University of New Mexico. In addition to selling her paintings as a professional artist, she works as a freelance illustrator and designer. As a community volunteer, she has had myriad memorable experiences with kids and is an active member of the PTA.

We encourage you to patronize your local bookstore. Most stores will order any title that they do not stock. You may also order directly from Mountain Press using the order form provided below or by calling our toll-free number and using your credit card. We will gladly send you a catalog upon request.

YOUNG ADULT

_____	Bold Women in Michigan's History	paper/$12.00
_____	Crazy Horse: A Photographic Biography	paper/$20.00
_____	Custer: A Photographic Biography	paper/$24.00
_____	Lewis and Clark: A Photographic Journey	paper/$18.00
_____	The Oregon Trail: A Photographic Journey	paper/$18.00
_____	The Pony Express: A Photographic History	paper/$22.00
_____	Sacagawea's Son: The Life of Jean Baptiste Charbonneau	paper/$10.00
_____	Smoky: The Cowhorse	paper/$16.00
_____	Stories of Young Pioneers: In Their Own Words	paper/$14.00

CHILDREN

_____	Awesome Osprey: Fishing Birds of the World	paper/$12.00
_____	The Charcoal Forest: How Fire Helps Animals and Plants	paper/$12.00
_____	Cowboy in the Making	cloth/$15.00
_____	Glacier National Park: An ABC Adventure	paper/$10.00
_____	Loons: Diving Birds of the North	paper/$12.00
_____	My First Horse	paper/$16.00
_____	Nature's Yucky! Gross Stuff That Helps Nature Work	paper/$10.00
_____	Nature's Yucky 2! The Desert Southwest	paper/$12.00
_____	Owls: Whoo Are They?	paper/$12.00
_____	Snowy Owls: Whoo Are They?	cloth/$12.00
_____	Spotted Bear: A Rocky Mountain Folktale	cloth/$15.00
_____	The Will James Cowboy Book	cloth/$18.00
_____	You Can Be a Nature Detective	paper/$14.00
_____	Young Cowboy	cloth/$15.00

Please include $3.00 for 1-4 books or $5.00 for 5 or more books for shipping and handling.

Send the books marked above. I enclose $ _____

Name _____

Address_____

City/State/Zip _____

☐ Payment enclosed (check or money order in U.S. funds)

Bill my: ☐ VISA ☐ MasterCard ☐ American Express ☐ Discover

Card No. _____ Exp. Date:_____

Security Code #_____ Signature _____

MOUNTAIN PRESS PUBLISHING COMPANY
P.O. Box 2399 • Missoula, MT 59806 • fax: 406-728-1635
Order Toll Free 1-800-234-5308 • *Have your credit card ready.*
e-mail: info@mtnpress.com • website: www.mountain-press.com